DAY OF THE DEAD
A First Look

KATIE PETERS

GRL Consultant, Diane Craig, Certified Literacy Specialist
Content Consultant, Bea Carrillo Hocker, Día de los Muertos Curriculum Expert and Museum Exhibit Curator

Lerner Publications ◆ Minneapolis

Educator Toolbox

Reading books is a great way for kids to express what they're interested in. Before reading this title, ask the reader these questions:

What do you think this book is about? Look at the cover for clues.

What do you already know about Day of the Dead?

What do you want to learn about Day of the Dead?

Let's Read Together

Encourage the reader to use the pictures to understand the text.

Point out when the reader successfully sounds out a word.

Praise the reader for recognizing sight words such as *who* and *of*.

TABLE OF CONTENTS

Day of the Dead 4

You Connect! 21
Social and Emotional Snapshot 22
Photo Glossary 23
Learn More 23
Index. 24

Day of the Dead

Day of the Dead is on November 1 and 2. It started in Mexico long ago.

Have you been to Mexico?

People think of loved ones who died. They think of good things about them.

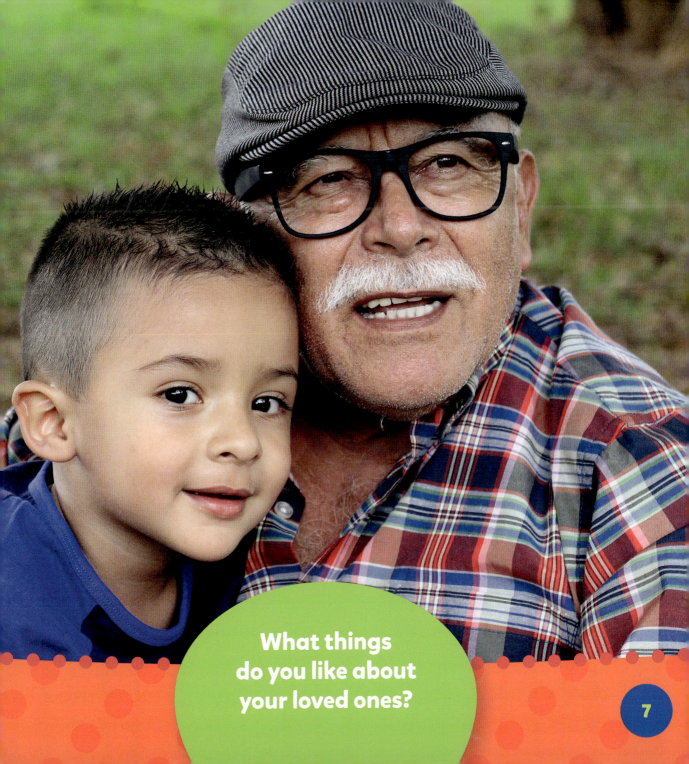

What things do you like about your loved ones?

Families build altars. They are for dead loved ones.

Families put pictures on altars.

They set out flowers and candles.

People put food on altars. There is sweet bread. There is food their loved ones liked.

What foods do you like?

Sugar skulls show that life is sweet.

People put names on them.
They set them on altars.

People visit the graves of loved ones.

There are parties and parades in the street.

People paint their faces.

Families share stories and music.
They must not forget to enjoy life.

You Connect!

Do you celebrate Day of the Dead?

What are some things you enjoy about life?

What is something you have done or would like to do for Day of the Dead?

Social and Emotional Snapshot

Student voice is crucial to building reader confidence. Ask the reader:

What is your favorite part of this book?

What is something you learned from this book?

Did this book remind you of any other holidays you celebrate?

Opportunities for social and emotional learning are everywhere. How can you connect the topic of this book to the SEL competencies below?

Self-Awareness
Relationship Skills
Social Awareness

Photo Glossary

altar

candles

grave

skulls

Learn More

Axelrod-Contrada, Joan. *Halloween and Day of the Dead Traditions around the World*. Mankato, MN: The Child's World, 2021.

Bullard, Lisa. *My Family Celebrates Day of the Dead*. Minneapolis: Lerner Publications, 2019.

Murray, Julie. *Day of the Dead*. Minneapolis: Abdo Publishing, 2018.

Index

altars, 8, 10, 12, 15

candles, 11

food, 12, 13

graves, 16

Mexico, 4, 5

pictures, 10

sugar skulls, 14

Photo Acknowledgments

The images in this book are used with the permission of: © Eve Orea/Shutterstock Images. pp. 4-5; © ajr_images/iStockphoto, pp. 6-7; © DarioGaona/iStockphoto, pp. 8-9; © betto rodrigues/Shutterstock Images, pp. 10, 23 (top left); © Cavan Images/iStockphoto, pp. 11, 23 (top right); © agcuesta/iStockphoto, p. 12; © Gogadicta/iStockphoto, pp. 12-13; © Suriel Ramzal/Shutterstock Images, pp. 14, 23 (bottom right); © Jose de Jesus Churion Del/Shutterstock Images, p. 15; © BeteMarques/iStockphoto, pp. 16-17, 23 (bottom left); © Quetzalcoatl1/Shutterstock Images, p. 18; © Simone Hogan/iStockphoto, p. 19; © Luciano Vettorato/iStockphoto, p. 20.

Cover Photo: © DarioGaona/iStockphoto.

Design Elements: © Mighty Media, Inc.

Copyright © 2023 by Lerner Publishing Group, Inc.

All rights reserved. International copyright secured. No part of this book may be reproduced, stored in a retrieval system, or transmitted in any form or by any means—electronic, mechanical, photocopying, recording, or otherwise—without the prior written permission of Lerner Publishing Group, Inc., except for the inclusion of brief quotations in an acknowledged review.

Lerner Publications Company
An imprint of Lerner Publishing Group, Inc.
241 First Avenue North
Minneapolis, MN 55401 USA

For reading levels and more information, look up this title at www.lernerbooks.com.

Main body text set in Mikado a Medium.
Typeface provided by Hannes von Doehren.

Library of Congress Cataloging-in-Publication Data

Names: Peters, Katie, author.
Title: Day of the Dead : a first look / Katie Peters.
Description: Minneapolis : Lerner Publications, 2023. | Series: Read about holidays. Read for a better world | Includes bibliographical references and index. | Audience: Ages 5-8 | Audience: Grades K-1 | Summary: "The Day of the Dead is a day to remember loved ones who died. Colorful photos and accessible text bring this family tradition to life for young learners"— Provided by publisher.
Identifiers: LCCN 2022010027 (print) | LCCN 2022010028 (ebook) | ISBN 9781728475615 (library binding) | ISBN 9781728478944 (paperback) | ISBN 9781728484068 (ebook)
Subjects: LCSH: All Souls' Day—Juvenile literature. | Mexico—Social life and customs—Juvenile literature.
Classification: LCC GT4995.A4 P478 2023 (print) | LCC GT4995.A4 (ebook) | DDC 394.266—dc23/eng/20220413

LC record available at https://lccn.loc.gov/2022010027
LC ebook record available at https://lccn.loc.gov/2022010028

Manufactured in the United States of America
1 - CG - 12/15/22